The 1896 Leadville
Ice Palace

The 1896 Leadville
Ice Palace

NOW YOU  KNOW MORE

Afton Rorvik

Filter Press, LLC
Westcliffe, Colorado

For Karl, Karol, Nali, and Florian.
How I love sharing this Colorado life with you!

The 1896 Leadville Ice Palace
Copyright © 2025 by Afton Rorvik
First edition

All rights reserved. Except for brief passages quoted in newspaper, magazine, radio, or television reviews, podcasts, and electronic media, no part of this book may be reproduced in any form or by any means, electronic or mechanical, without permission in writing from the publisher.

ISBN: (Paperback): 978-0-86541-266-8
ISBN: (Ebook): 978-0-86541-267-5

Library of Congress Control Number: 2025900144

Cover design: Jordan Ellender
Cover image: The ice palace by night and Mt. Elbert, courtesy of the Colorado Mountain History Collection, 01363pl.

Filter Press, LLC
Westcliffe, Colorado
https://www.FilterPressBooks.com/
719-481-2420
Info@FilterPressBooks.com

Contents

1 Leadville: The Magic City 1

2 A New Dream.............................. 6

3 The Ice Palace Begins 13

4 Parades, Clubs, and Costumes......... 20

5 Opening Day at Last 26

6 Months of Joy................................ 35

7 Another Ice Palace in Leadville?..... 42

Timeline 48

New Words... 50

Sources 53

Index 56

On January 2, 1896, *Leslie's Illustrated Newspaper* printed this sketch of the Leadville Ice Palace. It was drawn by F. H. Schnell.

By the bills that they throw out
  They've got a big blowout—
A palace that's built
  Out of huge chunks of ice—
They've got dancing and skating,
  And if half they're relating
Can be taken for true,
  They've got everything nice.

They've a swift way of joggin'
  Upon a toboggan—
A mile in a second,
  Or not more than two—
From the top to the bottom
  It's just like they shot 'em,
They give 'em a start
  And whiz-ziz! they are through.

Then there's riding and sliding
  And all kinds of gliding,
With carnivals, parties
  And masquerade balls:
With flash-lights a flashing
  And pretty girls "mashing"
And ice of all colors
  Mixed up in the walls.
    —by *Frank E. Vaughn*, published in
   The Herald Democrat, January 4, 1896

1 Leadville: The Magic City

John, Charles, and Patrick Gallagher had a dream. They wanted to get rich. Really rich!

Their dream started in Ireland. They heard stories of people finding gold and then silver in the Rocky Mountains of Colorado. They had to go! So in 1876, these three brothers packed their bags and boarded a ship to travel to America.

After many weeks, the ship reached the United States. Then the Gallaghers traveled on trains and by horseback until they finally arrived in Colorado.

They bought tools and animals (**mules**, burros, and horses) that would help them pull gold and silver from the mountains. Then they began the steep climb into the mountains, just below the clouds. They climbed to almost

The 1896 Leadville Ice Palace

Leslie's Illustrated Newspaper featured this sketch by E. Jump on the front page of the April 12, 1879 edition. The caption reads, "Colorado—our wonderful mineral productions—hauling machinery in the mountains, near the timber line, at Leadville, 10,500 feet above the level of the sea."

10,500 feet above sea level.

In this high place they started mining. They used tools and animals to dig deep holes in the mountains and pulled out buckets of dirt and rock. They crushed the rock and searched through what they had unearthed. After months of hard work in an ice-cold winter, they hit **pay dirt**.

Silver! Silver! They became rich. Really rich! Their dream came true. News spread quickly. Thousands of people began to come to this place high in the mountains of Colorado.

More people came from Ireland. Others came from Germany, Sweden, England, Scotland, and Spain.

Everyone wanted to strike it rich.

What a place! The town needed a name. Some early **miners** called the area California

---

Know More!
How Did Miners Find Gold and Silver?

Miners in the 1800s used many different tools and methods to find gold and silver. In rivers, they did **placer mining.** They ran water through pans, screens, and other devices to separate gold flakes and nuggets from rocks and dirt.

In a process called **hard-rock mining,** they used drills, hammers, and **dynamite** to remove gold and silver ore from mine shafts.

The 1896 Leadville Ice Palace

Leslie's Illustrated Newspaper printed this image of Leadville, Colorado on April 12, 1879.

Gulch. Others called it the Cloud City because the town was so high in the mountains that clouds often covered it.

In 1878, town leaders decided on a name: Leadville. They chose the name because the town had lots of **lead carbonate**, a black sand that had silver in it. Soon the mountain town had a post office, a bank, a hotel, a church, a hospital, and many houses.

A man named Horace Tabor owned a general store and made a lot of money by **grubstaking miners**. He gave them supplies and food in exchange for part ownership of their mines and anything they discovered. That meant that when miners found silver and made a lot of money, so did Horace Tabor.

Soon Horace Tabor had many mines and a lot of money. In 1879, he decided to build an **opera house**, and he named it the Tabor Opera House. Big cities like New York and San Francisco had opera houses. Why shouldn't Leadville have one too?

Some people started calling Leadville "the Magic City," because it could make people like the Gallagher brothers, Horace Tabor, and others very rich, unbelievably fast. Dreams of getting rich magically seemed to come true in Leadville, Colorado.

At least for a few years.

The Tabor Opera House was built in just 100 days. The showman Buffalo Bill visited it. So did some live tigers. Some say magician Harry Houdini performed there, but then he disappeared.

2 A New Dream

Gold, silver, and lead all brought dreamers to Leadville, Colorado. These people liked to think big. They dreamed of big mines, big buildings, and big bank accounts.

Then, in 1893, life changed in Leadville.

That year the United States government ended the **Sherman Silver Purchase Act**. This law had made the government buy lots of silver at a set price. When the law ended, the cost of digging silver from mines in the Rocky Mountains was more than the amount people would pay for silver.

Mines closed. Many people lost their jobs. Lots of people left Leadville.

City leaders started to talk. They asked themselves how they could bring back the magic and people to Leadville.

A New Dream

Someone started dreaming about building a palace made out of ice because people in other cities had built ice palaces.

The people of Leadville began to talk about how an ice palace and a winter carnival would bring people and joy back to Leadville.

In 1895, the people of Leadville decided an ice palace was just what the town needed. If they could build the best ice palace ever, travelers would visit Leadville.

They would buy from stores and stay in hotels. They would eat at Leadville restaurants. Maybe some of them would even decide to stay. Most importantly, the ice palace would give jobs to unemployed miners who really needed work.

Of course, a party at an ice palace would be a lot of fun. Plus, building an ice palace would show the world that Leadville would not die.

Because people in Leadville liked to dream big, they decided to build the biggest and the best ice palace the world had ever seen.

City leaders put notices in newspapers. They needed an **architect** to plan their ice palace. They hired Charles E. Joy because he had designed the 1888 Minnesota Ice Palace.

The 1896 Leadville Ice Palace

In 1884, Alexander Cowper Hutchinson planned the Montreal Ice Palace (above). In 1888, people in Minnesota hired Charles E. Joy to design their ice palace (below).

A New Dream

Charles Joy started making drawings of the Leadville Ice Palace. It would look like a full-sized castle and measure 450 feet long and 320 feet wide. That is about as long as one and a half football fields and as wide as two.

> ### Know More!
> ### How Did People Talk to Each Other in 1895?
>
> People in 1895 did not text, email, or have social media. They did not use FaceTime or Zoom. They did not have cellphones. But they had many other ways to communicate.
>
> - They wrote letters. The first post office in Leadville started in 1877. By 1880, the Leadville Post Office handled almost six thousand letters every day.
> - They read newspapers. They could read about news and people, and they could find out about jobs and things for sale. By 1895, Leadville had five newspapers.
> - They sent messages by **telegraph**. They typed messages in **Morse code** and then sent them over electric wires.
> - They used a shared telephone. The first telephone came to Leadville in 1879.

The 1896 Leadville Ice Palace

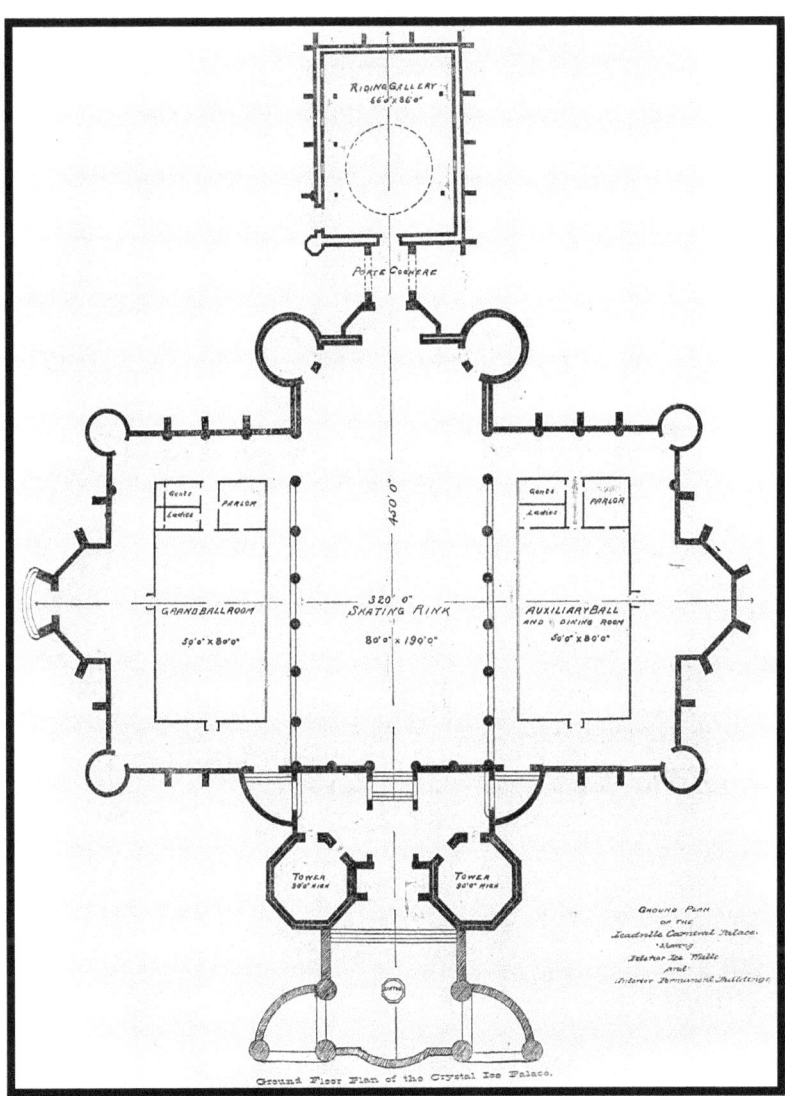

This is an initial floorplan Charles Joy proposed for the Leadville Ice Palace. In this early plan, the ice palace would have a riding gallery, a grand ballroom, a skating rink, an auxiliary ball and dining room, two ninety-foot-high towers, and a grand entryway.

A New Dream

Thinking as big as Leadville city leaders, Charles Joy designed the ice palace to have high walls and high towers, including a **toboggan** run from the top of one of the towers. Inside would be a dining hall, a skating rink, and a **ballroom** to dance in. A small building outside the ice palace would have a merry-go-round.

Charles Joy created a design that required workers to build an inside frame of wood with a roof. The outside walls and many of the interior walls would be made of ice blocks.

In November 1895, city leaders approved the final building plans drawn by Charles Joy. They dreamed of celebrating Christmas Day at the Leadville Ice Palace, but first they had to build the huge structure.

Charles Joy was an architect, but Leadville needed someone to take charge of raising money and directing the workers who would build the palace. Edwin W. Senior tried, but he could not get people to give money to help pay for building it.

Soon Leadville asked Tingley S. Wood. He ran a mine and knew how to work hard and raise money. Director Wood got people to give

The 1896 Leadville Ice Palace

Director Tingley S. Wood (left) and architect Charles E. Joy (right)

money so the ice palace could be built. He also gave a lot of his own money to build the ice palace.

It was November 1895. Could they really build it before Christmas?

3 The Ice Palace Begins

Soon, lots of noise filled the air in Leadville. By November 1895, the boom of exploding dynamite on Leadville's Capitol Hill rattled windows. Workers cut trees and blasted the stumps off the hill to make room for the ice palace.

Workers and wagons full of lumber came to Leadville. Builders used this lumber to assemble the outside frame and roof of the ice palace. Men with hammers banged and banged nails into wood. Around the frame workers made a 20-foot-wide walkway from wood. They planned to stack ice blocks outside that wooden walkway.

The group in charge of the ice palace put

The 1896 Leadville Ice Palace

> **The Leadville Ice Palace and Carnival Association—Notice to Ice Men!**
>
> Bids will be received by the undersigned up to October 10, 1895, for the cutting and delivering to the site of from 2,000 to 4,000 tons of ice for the erection of an ice palace as soon as weather permits. Blocks to be cut say 22x24 inches and one foot thick. Ice must be clear and free of dirt. Right reserved to reject any or all bids.
>
> By Order of the Directors.
> W. L. Temple, Secretary, Rooms 3 and 4, Iron building.

Advertisement in *The Herald Democrat* on October 15, 1895

advertisements into newspapers to find people to cut and deliver ice. Sled drivers and tired horses went back and forth, day and night. Each sled carried ragged chunks of ice cut from ponds and nearby lakes.

Workers used axes and saws to cut the ice into blocks to make the walls of the ice palace. Leadville's Capitol Hill now looked like an ant hill. Workers covered the hill and made lots of noise.

On November 25, 1895, Charles Joy placed the first block of ice outside the wooden frame. That block measured 20 inches wide and 30 inches long, but it was only 13 inches thick. That unlucky number made Director Wood nervous.

The Ice Palace Begins

Workers added other blocks of ice and poured water between the blocks. When the water froze, it connected the blocks together. *The Herald Democrat*, a Leadville newspaper, reported on November 26, 1895, that the workers used boiling water, which "freezes quicker than cold water." The newspaper also reported that the water "escaping down the walls freezes on its way to the ground, making the walls thicker at the base than they are at the top."

An 1882 birds-eye view of the town of Leadville drawn by Henry Wellge. The Leadville Ice Palace was built on Capitol Hill in the 400 block between West Seventh and Eighth Streets. The arrow shows the approximate location.

Know More!
Does Boiling Water Really Freeze Faster Than Cold Water?

In 1963, Tanzanian teenager Erasto Mpemba made a batch of ice cream that created waves in the physics world. He showed that sometimes hot liquids froze faster than cold liquids, something Leadville Ice Palace builders knew about in 1896. Mpemba's findings became known as the Mpemba effect.

If you live in a cold climate, you can (with an adult's help) do your own ice palace experiment to find out if boiling water freezes fastest.

- Make some ice cubes in your freezer.
- Take the ice cubes outside (in cold weather) and build two small ice cube buildings that look the same.
- Boil some water and gently pour it over one building.
- Pour the same amount of cold water over the other building.
- Keep track of the time it takes for the ice cubes in each building to freeze together.
- What did your experiment show? Can you vary the experiment? What happens if you use warm water? Or bigger ice cubes?

The Ice Palace Begins

The Leadville Ice Palace under construction

The ice walls grew taller and taller, but then something unexpected happened in Leadville. Unusually warm weather blew into the Cloud City.

One day the temperature was 35 degrees Fahrenheit (1.7 degrees Celsius), but the next day the temperature rose to 65 degrees Fahrenheit (18.3 degrees Celsius). No one could believe it. Suddenly, it felt like spring in Leadville.

Director Wood felt nervous again. He could

not make or pay a cold wind blow into Leadville. And he could not just sit and watch the palace melt away. He had to do something. He decided to buy lots and lots of **muslin,** a kind of fabric, and "dress" the palace.

Construction of the Leadville Ice Palace with muslin draped over the walls

The Ice Palace Begins

During the day, the ice palace wore muslin to protect it from the sun. In the evening, when the temperature got colder, the workers took the fabric down. At night, the fire department sprayed the walls with water, and workers kept laying ice blocks.

Finally, those warm temperatures blew right out of Leadville. Now Director Wood could smile again. Or could he? Days later, more warm weather blew into town. This time, Director Wood remained calm and pulled out his muslin again.

Architect Joy told a reporter that the ice palace walls would stay together even if they shrank to 10 inches thick. On December 21, 1895, *The Herald Democrat* reported Joy's prediction: "The Ice Palace might last until the Fourth of July."

The warm weather seemed to know that it was not welcome in Leadville. It did not stay more than a few days. Once again, it became cold in Leadville.

Perfect ice palace weather! But could workers finish the palace in time for Christmas?

4
Parades, Clubs, and Costumes

Everyone in Leadville talked about the ice palace that winter of 1895. Some talked about the progress on the outside as they watched the walls and towers grow tall.

Some people wondered about the inside of the palace. What kind of displays was Director Wood planning? He had hired Phillip Kelly, an ice **sculptor**, to do something, but what?

On December 6, 1895, *The Herald Democrat*, one of Leadville's newspapers, reported, "The Crystal Palace museum has been kept a dead secret and Director General Wood has kept his modeler in the Ice Palace studio under lock and key."

According to *The Herald Democrat* on December 18, 1895, some people said workers were "freezing things like sewing machines and pickles into ice blocks" for display inside the palace. The reporter wondered, "Are they trying to show people what they can buy in Leadville?"

By December 21, 1895, *The Herald Democrat* added to the excitement by printing, "The ball and banqueting rooms will be heated by eight large hard **coal baseburners** that have been set in their places."

The streets of Leadville filled with stories about the ice palace. Banners and flags in the ice palace colors of red, white, and blue waved all over town.

Signs everywhere announced the Leadville Ice Palace in bold red paint. Each sign reminded the town about the parties, parades, and celebrations that would happen as soon as the ice palace opened. The town had called these celebrations the **Crystal Carnival.**

The people of Leadville prepared for their ice palace, working hard to make their town look good. Some people painted their houses inside and out. Some fixed up a bedroom to rent to visitors.

The 1896 Leadville Ice Palace   22

> Your aunts and cousins will all be here to the Ice Palace opening. Paper your rooms and show them you don't live in a dug-out.   J. D. Thomas & Son, 107 East Fourth street.

Advertisement in *The Herald Democrat* on December 13, 1895

In preparation for the Crystal Carnival events, townspeople formed hockey, ice skating, toboggan, and skiing clubs. Each club created special costumes, which often included matching socks and hats.

Almost every day, the streets of Leadville

Earnestine Kuehl in her ice palace costume (left) and an unnamed ice skater in his costume (right)

Parades, Clubs, and Costumes

were filled with parades. Bands, floats, and smiling people all seemed to say, "Don't forget! The ice palace is coming soon. Get ready!"

The high ice walls continued to grow. People could now see a statue named **Lady Leadville**, made by Phillip Kelly, standing tall at the north entrance of the ice palace. This 19-foot snow and ice woman wore a crown on her head and a flowing dress. Over one arm she carried a scroll with $200,000,000 written on it

This photograph of the Leadville Ice Palace taken in 1896 by William Henry Jackson

The 1896 Leadville Ice Palace

The main entrance of Leadville's ice palace with the Lady Leadville ice sculpture.

in gold numbers. That was the amount of money Leadville mines had earned up until the year 1894.

The town of Leadville had never looked better. Joy and pride showed on people's faces

Parades, Clubs, and Costumes

as they talked about their parades, clubs, and costumes.

But one little problem worried everyone. Christmas came and went, and the workers had not finished the palace.

Would they *ever* finish the ice palace? When would the people of Leadville be able to see inside?

5 Opening Day at Last

On New Year's Day 1896, the streets of Leadville filled with people. Today was the day! The Leadville Ice Palace would finally open.

The grand, cold opening day began with a parade, led by the town's police. Next came a little girl waving to the crowd from her papa's sled, pulled by two pug dogs. The Fort Dodge Cowboy Band followed with their large drum hauled by donkeys. Then came members of the Snowshoe Club, in matching costumes made from white blankets. Others followed, including the Toboggan Ladies, dressed in red.

Director Tingley S. Wood led the members of the Ice Palace Planning Group, followed by

Opening Day at Last

Opening day parade on Harrison Avenue in Leadville on January 1, 1896

a large cluster of children in costumes. Firemen followed.

Finally, the men who helped build the ice palace marched down the street. They pulled sleds made of wood with blocks of ice on them, like the ones used in the palace walls. They also carried some of their tools, such as saws and axes. Some of them proudly carried a sign that read, "We Helped Build the Ice Palace."

On the streets of Leadville, parade watchers, dressed in costumes of their own, cheered

The 1896 Leadville Ice Palace

and whistled. They joined the end of the parade.

The parade went uphill and stopped right in front of the east entrance to the ice palace. The north entrance with the statue of Lady Leadville was not yet finished.

Sunlight bounced off the palace walls and made the castle sparkle.

People walked under the shining ice arches and finally went inside their ice palace. They saw with their own eyes what they had been reading about in the newspapers.

Sunlight glittered off the walls and towers of the Leadville Ice Palace with Lady Leadville in front

Opening Day at Last

Phillip Kelly made sculptures of miners, women, animals, and many interesting objects

They discovered frozen statues of miners. Phillip Kelly had made the statues in a shed behind the ice palace. He had collected snow and then mixed it with water to freeze it. As the snow and water froze, he shaped the statues. Then he rubbed water over them to make them shine.

As visitors walked on, they found ice blocks with products from Leadville shops inside. They saw butter, fish, cans of **oysters,** and other items enclosed in clear ice.

The 1896 Leadville Ice Palace

Know More!
How Do You Freeze Something into a Large Block of Ice?

The people of Leadville wanted visitors to buy things in town. Director Wood decided to advertise by freezing goods inside large blocks of ice. Here's how they froze the objects in ice:

- They placed each item in a large tank and held it in place with white thread.
- They filled the tank with water.
- They needed to keep the ice clear, so people could see the objects inside. To do this, they let the water freeze slowly, by controlling the outside temperature. It took two to three days to freeze each 400-pound block.

Try freezing something into a block of ice yourself. Is it easy to keep the ice clear? Can you see the white thread?

Opening Day at Last

They walked past exhibits with stuffed Colorado wildlife.

Farther inside, they saw something that took their breath away.

Clear ice shone from the floor of a skating rink. Ice frosting covered wooden beams on the ceiling, and little icicles hung from the beams and sparkled like diamonds.

Ice pillars, with colored lights hidden inside them, lined the walls. The lights made the pillars glow: Yellow. Green. Blue. More colored lights hung from the ceiling. Others filled the

The Leadville Ice Palace skating rink had a trussed wooden roof. Bell-shaped chandeliers with multicolored electric lights in their globes hung 14 feet above the ice. Photo by William Henry.

The 1896 Leadville Ice Palace

> **Know More!**
> **How Did Workers Put Lights Inside the Ice Pillars in the Skating Rink?**
>
> The ice pillars around the ice rink were five feet on each side. Workers dangled various colors of **incandescent light bulbs** inside the hollow pillars.
>
> Some people today use bulbs like this in their houses and call them "Edison bulbs" after Thomas Edison, who invented them.

corners. Color bounced from ice block to ice block all around the room. The lights made the space magical, especially since most people didn't have electricity in their homes at that time!

People discovered two rooms on either side of the skating rink. These rooms had wooden floors, **coal-burning stoves**, and dressing rooms for skaters. One was a ballroom where people could dance, and the other was both a ballroom and a dining room. Both rooms had glass walls so people could stay warm and still watch the ice skaters.

The Leadville Ice Palace skating rink as pictured in the January 5, 1896, *Rocky Mountain News*

After the townsfolk saw the skating rink, Director Wood invited everyone into one of the ballrooms. Leadville mayor S. D. Nicholson and a few other people gave speeches. Then Director Wood smiled and said in a booming voice, "The carnival is now open. Enjoy yourselves."

The people of Leadville had been waiting and waiting. At last, their ice palace was open. They spent that evening skating and dancing

The 1896 Leadville Ice Palace

until late into the night. Some even took toboggan rides from one tall tower.

Everyone agreed, "This is the best ice palace ever!"

But the ice palace was *still* not finished. After everyone left, workers hurried back into the palace to make the final additions.

The Leadville Ice Palace toboggan as pictured in the January 5, 1896, *Rocky Mountain News*. One of the men pictured is Director Wood. Can you tell which one?
(Hint: Look at the men's chins.)

6 Months of Joy

Workers finally laid the last block of ice on January 15, 1896. No more work on the Leadville Ice Palace—now just fun!

To celebrate the completion of the Leadville Ice Palace, newspaper reporters from all over Colorado were invited to Leadville to see and experience the ice palace. January 15 was Press Day at the ice palace. The Leadville mayor issued a **proclamation**: "Anyone on the streets on January 15th from 2 pm to 10 pm MUST wear a costume."

Men, women, and children dressed in fancy costumes. One woman made a dress from newspaper and white fur and won a gold medal for it.

That day, visitors walked past the Lady Leadville statue. She seemed to wave them inside. They pushed through **turnstiles** at the

> * * *
> Hold your breath—Press day am a-coming.
> * * *
> . Timid people had better get down to a lower altitude on Press day.
> * * *
> The mayor's proclamation is awaited with a holy hush. It may cause a holy terror.
> * * *
> The press gang have secured a barrel of ham fat to grease the toboggan slide on Press day.
> * * *

Advice to the people of Leadville regarding Press Day, as reported in *The Herald Democrat* on January 9, 1896

just-opened north entrance and then climbed icy stairs into the frozen palace.

All afternoon and evening, special events happened: a 1-mile race with a prize of $50, skating races, a hockey game, and in the evening a masquerade ball and skating carnival.

Press Day spread the word about the ice palace. Newspaper reporters from all over the United States wrote about Leadville's amazing castle of ice and its winter carnival.

A January 16, 1896, article in *The Colorado Daily Chieftain* from Pueblo stated, "It is one of the finest ice castles ever built in the world."

This article and others encouraged visitors, just as Leadville townspeople had hoped.

Every day after Press Day, people danced and skated in the ice palace. Adults paid 50¢ (about $18 in 2025 dollars) and children paid 25¢ (about $9 in 2025 dollars) to visit the ice palace. People came to Leadville from all over Colorado to see the amazing palace and to enjoy the festivities. They even came from cities as far away as New York and Chicago.

One day the Leadville Ice Palace opened just for miners. The day started with a parade (of course). Then the miners took turns to see how fast they could drill a hole in a huge piece of rock. Leadville miners were the fastest.

On February 8, 1896, the ice palace celebrated Children's Day. Public schools closed and children played games and skated inside the ice palace.

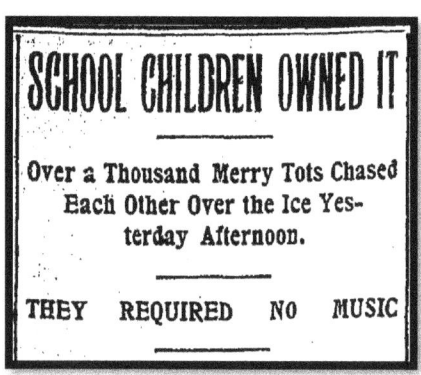

Herald Democrat headline, February 8, 1896

The 1896 Leadville Ice Palace

38

Music was a big part of the festivities at the Leadville Ice Palace. Bands and musicians came from all over to march in parades and to play in the ice palace ballrooms. Denver's First Regiment Band marched in a January 8, 1896, parade and performed in the East Ballroom.

For three months, the people of Leadville and their visitors played at the ice palace, danced, and heard lots of musical concerts.

People who lived close to Leadville could walk to the ice palace. Others rode horses or took **sleigh** rides to the palace.

People who lived farther away in Colorado or in another state came to Leadville on trains.

> **Leadville Ice Palace and Crystal Carnival**
>
> Opens Jan. 4. For this occasion the Denver and Rio Grande railroad will place tickets on sale Jan. 3 and 4 at rate of $5.00 the round trip, including two admissions to the Ice Palace. Special train will leave Denver Jan. 3, 11:00 p. m. and returning, leave Leadville Jan. 5, 11:00 p. m. Arrangements have been made for $5.00 round trip Pullman rate; this allows the holders of tickets to occupy berths in sleeper while in Leadville. Berths can be reserved to-day at the City ticket office, 1662 Larimer st.

A Rio Grande railroad advertisement from the January 2, 1896, *Rocky Mountain News*

Trains charged $5 (about $190 in 2025 dollars) for a round-trip ticket from Denver to Leadville. The ticket price included one night in a train **sleeper car** and admission to the ice palace.

What a winter it was in Leadville, Colorado! But winter would not last forever. By March the sun began warming the mountains. The ice palace began to melt. Workers fixed some walls, but soon other walls melted.

Townsfolk remembered Charles Joy's prediction about the Leadville Ice Palace. Could it really last until the Fourth of July? By the end of March, it looked like Joy was wrong.

The 1896 Leadville Ice Palace

Know More!
What Were Trains Like in 1896?

The train between Denver and Leadville was a **narrow-gauge train**, meaning the train tracks were closer together than tracks used today. The narrow tracks made it easier for trains to climb up into the mountains, but during winter, snow often stopped the trains. Passengers were stranded, and workers had to shovel snow off the tracks.

Today, Leadville offers a two-and-a-half-hour train ride on part of the original route.

A train with a rotary snowplow clears snow off the tracks at Hagerman Pass. This pass is west of Leadville and crosses the Continental Divide.

The sun kept shining in Leadville, and the ice palace kept melting. Director Tingley S. Wood put a fence around the palace to keep melting ice from falling on people. The group in charge of the ice palace finally voted to close it on March 28.

That night, townspeople watched red fireworks light up the tall towers. They remembered the icy stairs that led to the skating rink filled with lights. They laughed about the pickles in ice blocks. They talked about the costumes, the sports clubs, the contests, and all the parades. They reminded each other of the muslin Director Wood had used when the warm weather came to Leadville.

Townspeople walked home that night with sad hearts. The Crystal Carnival was over. The Leadville Ice Palace was melting away. But no one could forget the joy of the past few months.

The ice palace had brought Leadville alive with music, color, and fun. Everyone agreed that Leadville had truly built the biggest and best ice palace ever!

7 Another Ice Palace in Leadville?

Soon the people of Leadville could easily see the wooden frame inside their ice palace. Everyone wondered: What should happen now?

Earlier in the year, newspapers had made different suggestions. On February 29, 1896, *The Leadville Daily/Evening Chronicle* had printed a story titled "Bombard the Palace," proposing that for a "Grand Wind-up of the Carnival," miners should dynamite the structure and "in one fell swoop raze to the ground the outer walls of Leadville's marvelous palace of beauty."

Miners in Leadville liked to use dynamite.

Some people had suggested covering the ice with hay so it wouldn't melt. Others wanted to let the ice melt but save the frame and build

Another Ice Palace in Leadville?

another ice palace the following year. The January 15, 1896, *Leadville Daily/Evening Chronical* had suggested that the ice palace grounds should become a park with a statue of Tingley S. Wood, the man who took charge of building the Leadville Ice Palace and never knew the word *fail*.

Everyone in Leadville had hoped the ice palace would help the town, and it did for three months. Visitors came to Leadville and bought things. They stayed at hotels and ate at restaurants.

As the winter ended, the ice palace melted. The streets around Ice Palace Hill filled with water and mud.

Then, in the summer of 1896, something happened in Leadville that made people stop talking about the ice palace. The miners went on **strike**. They said they would not work again until they got higher pay. The miners and mine owners fought in the streets of Leadville. In September 1896, soldiers from Colorado's National Guard came to Leadville.

These soldiers took some of the lumber from the ice palace. They used it to make shelters where they could eat and sleep. Slowly the rest

The 1896 Leadville Ice Palace

The Colorado National Guard built Camp McIntire near Leadville, using wood from the ice palace

of the ice palace frame disappeared. No more ice palace. Not even a wooden frame.

Still, the people of Leadville did not forget their ice palace. The Leadville Heritage Museum and the National Mining Hall of Fame and Museum in Leadville made displays about the ice palace. People donated photos, ice skates, and other items from 1896. Both museums have models of the ice palace. Frank Goris built one out of foam. Jeff Wrona built another from plastic.

Another Ice Palace in Leadville?

Items from the ice palace on display in the Leadville Heritage Museum: an ice hook (left) and Leadville belt buckles (right)

Model of the Leadville Ice Palace made by Frank Goris, showing the internal wooden frames

The 1896 Leadville Ice Palace

In addition, every March, Leadville still celebrates with a Crystal Carnival. Residents don't build an ice palace, but they do have contests with horses and skis.

Some people have talked of building another ice palace, but no one has built one yet.

Who knows what might happen in Leadville? This little town so high in the Colorado mountains still has many stories to tell.

> **Know More!**
> **How Much Did It Cost to Build the Leadville Ice Palace?**
>
> Building the Leadville Ice Palace was expensive. The builders, sculptors, ice haulers, and other workers needed to be paid. No one is certain how much it cost to build the ice palace, but some have made guesses:
>
> - On February 20, 1896, *The Daily Journal* from Telluride reported that it had cost $42,000 (about $1.5 million in 2025 dollars).
> - Darlene Godat Weir, in her book *Leadville's Ice Palace: A Colossus in the Colorado Rockies*, claimed it had cost $65,000 (about $2.4 million in 2025 dollars).
> - On February 9, 1947, *The Rocky Mountain News* from Denver reported that it had cost $140,000 (about $5.1 million in 2025 dollars).

Timeline

1860 — Gold is discovered in California Gulch, one mile east of current-day Leadville.

1861 — Colorado becomes a territory.

1876 — The Gallagher brothers (John, Charles, and Patrick) come to Leadville from Ireland.

1876 — Colorado becomes the thirty-eighth state in the United States.

1877 — Silver is discovered in Leadville.

1877 — Leadville gets a post office.

1878 — The town is officially called Leadville.

1878 — Leadville gets a newspaper.

1879 — The "silver secret" is out. Thousands of people come to Leadville to find more silver.

1879 — Horace Tabor builds the Leadville Opera House.

1879 — Tabor brings the first telephone to Leadville.

1880 — The first railroad comes to Leadville.

1880 — The first school is built in Leadville.

1881 — Electricity comes to Leadville.

Timeline

1890—The Sherman Silver Purchase Act becomes law.

1893—The Sherman Silver Purchase Act is repealed.

1896 (January 1)—The Leadville Ice Palace opens.

1896 (March 28)—The Leadville Ice Palace closes.

1896—Miners go on strike in Leadville.

1896—The Colorado National Guard comes to Leadville and sets up Camp McIntire.

New Words

architect: a person who designs buildings and helps them get built. Architect Charles Joy knew how to build with ice.

ballroom: a room made for dancing

coal baseburner or coal-burning stove: an iron stove that burns coal for heat. The coal looks like a black rock. People today still burn coal for heat and power.

Crystal Carnival: an event first celebrated on January 1, 1896, Leadville, Colorado. The town still has a Crystal Carnival every year.

dynamite: a mixture made mostly of nitroglycerin that is used to blow up rocks for mining

grubstaking: providing miners with tools and supplies in exchange for a share of the profits from a mine

hard-rock mining: using drills, hammers, and dynamite to get rocks out of the earth. Miners hope the mined rocks have silver or gold in them.

incandescent light bulb: a light bulb whose light comes from wire heated with an electric charge

Lady Leadville: a statue in Leadville made of ice and snow. She stood in front of the ice palace and was

New Words

almost as tall as the palace walls.

lead carbonate: heavy black sand that miners found, and discarded, when they looked for gold in the 1800s. Only later did they discover it contained silver and was valuable.

miner: a person who drills and digs in mines. Early miners in Colorado worked in unsafe and dark spaces, often earning only a little bit of money every day.

Morse code: a code in which electrical signals stand for letters. In the 1800s, people sent messages in Morse code over telegraph wires. The code was named for inventor Samuel Morse.

mule: an animal that is half horse and half donkey

muslin: a plain, light, white cotton fabric

narrow-gauge train: a train that ran on tracks that were closer together than those used by modern trains. Narrow-gauge train engines and cars were also smaller than modern versions.

opera house: a theater where people can see operas and other shows

oyster: an edible shellfish

pay dirt: earth filled with gold and silver that produces a profit for a miner

The 1896 Leadville Ice Palace

placer mining: using water to flush out gold from rocks and dirt near rivers

proclamation: an announcement of something very important

sculptor: an artist who makes three-dimensional works of art

Sherman Silver Purchase Act: a law passed by the U.S. Congress in 1890. It required the government to buy a certain amount of silver at a set price.

sleeper car: a train car with beds for passengers

sleigh: a sled drawn by a horse with iron runners for traveling over snow in the winter

strike: when workers refuse to do their jobs until business owners agree to give them better pay, shorter work hours, or a safer place to work

telegraph: a system for sending messages over electric wires

toboggan: a long, narrow, flat-bottomed sled made of a thin board curved upward and backward at the front

turnstile: a mechanical gate with horizontal arms that allows only one person to enter at a time

Sources

Books

Blair, Edward. *Leadville: Colorado's Magic City*. Boulder, CO: Fred Pruett Books, 1980.

Blair, Edward. *Palace of Ice: A History of Leadville's Ice Palace 1895-1896*. Leadville, CO: Timberline Books, Ltd., 1977.

Buys, Christian. *A Quick History of Leadville*. Lake City, CO: Western Reflections Publishing, 2007.

Buys, Christian. *Leadville: Colorado's Magic City*. Boulder, CO: Fred Pruett Books, 1980.

Coquoz, Rene L. *King Pleasure Reigned in 1896: The Story of the Fabulous Leadville Ice Palace*, 4th ed. Boulder, CO: Johnson Publishing Company, 1986.

Downey, Matthew T. and Fay D. Metcalf. *Colorado: Crossroads of the West*, 3rd ed. Boulder, CO: Pruett Publishing Company, 1999.

Larsh, Ed B. and Robert Nichols. *Leadville U.S.A.* Boulder, CO: Johnson Books, 1993.

Smith, Duane A. *Horace Tabor: His Life and the Legend*. Boulder, CO: University Press of Colorado, 1989.

Weir, Darlene Godat. *Leadville's Ice Palace: A Colossus in

the Colorado Rockies. Lakewood, CO: Ice Castle Editions, 1994.

Transcript

Weir, Darlene. "The Leadville Ice Palace, a Slide Presentation." Lake County Library, July 17, 1986. Transcribed by Susan A. Wold.

Web Materials

Britannica.com. "The Silver Issue." https://www.britannica.com/place/United-States/The-Sherman-Antitrust-Act#ref612938.

Colorado Central Magazine, "The Leadville Ice Palace — A Look Back." December 1, 2009. https://www.coloradocentralmagazine.com/the-leadville-ice-palace-a-look-back/.

Colorado Encyclopedia.
   https://coloradoencyclopedia.org/.

Colorado State Library. Historic Newspapers. https://www.coloradohistoricnewspapers.org/.

Colorado Tourism Office. "Leadville Ski Joring and Crystal Carnival Weekend." https://www.colorado.com/leadville/events/history-heritage-events/leadville-ski-joring-crystal-carnival-weekend.

Sources

Frank Leslie's Illustrated Newspaper. "The New Eldorado: Leadville: The Great Mining Center of Colorado." April 12, 1879. https://archive.org/details/sim_leslies-weekly_1879-04-12_48_1228.

Herald Democrat. "Leadville's Museums." 2022. https://www.leadvilleherald.com/special_editions/heritage/page_811de0f9-ab9d-5631-8925-8c178df1cb31.html.

Leadville.com. "A Timeline of Leadville's History." https://leadville.com/a-time-line-of-leadvilles-history/.

Williams, George Wallace. "The Leadville Ice Palace." *Leslie's Weekly Illustrated.* January 2, 1896. https://archive.org/details/sim_leslies-weekly_1896-01-02_82_2103/mode/2up.

Index

architect, 11, 12, 19, 50
ballroom, 10, 11, 32, 38, 50
California Gulch, 3, 4, 48
Capitol Hill, 13, 14, 15
Cloud City, 4, 17
coal baseburners, 21, 50
coal-burning stoves, 32, 50
Colorado's National Guard, 43, 44, 49
Cost to enter Leadville Ice Palace, 37
Crystal Carnival, 21, 22, 41, 46, 50, 54
Denver's First Regiment Band, 38
dynamite, 3, 13, 42, 50
February 8, 1896 Children's Day at Leadville Ice Palace, 37
Fort Dodge Cowboy Band, 26
Gallagher, Charles, John, and Patrick, 1, 5, 48
Goris, Frank Ice palace model builder, 44, 45
grubstaking, 4, 50

hard-rock mining, 3, 50
Hutchinson, Alexander Cowper, 1884 Montreal Ice Palace Designer, 8
Ice Palace Planning Group, 26
incandescent light bulb, 32, 50
January 15, 1896 Leadville Ice Palace is completed, 35, 43
Joy, Charles E, architect of the Leadville Ice Palace, 2, 7, 8, 9, 10, 11, 12, 14, 19, 39, 50
Kelly, Phillip Ice Sculptor, 20, 23, 29
Lady Leadville, 23, 24, 28, 35, 50
lead carbonate, 4, 51
Leadville Heritage Museum, 22, 44, 45, 58
Leadville Ice Palace cost, 47
lumber, 13, 43
Magic City, 1, 3, 5, 53
miner, 2, 3, 4, 7, 29, 37, 42, 43, 49, 50, 51

Index

Minnesota Ice Palace, 7, 8
Morse code, 9, 51
Montreal Ice Palace, 8
Mpemba effect, 16
mule, 1, 51
muslin, 18, 19, 41, 51
narrow-gauge train, 40, 51
National Mining Hall of Fame and Museum, 44
Nicholson, S. D.
  Leadville mayor, 33
opera house, 5, 48, 52
oyster, 29, 51
parade, 20, 23, 25, 26, 27, 28, 37, 38, 41
pay dirt, 3, 51
placer mining, 3, 52
Press Day, 35, 36, 37
proclamation, 35, 52
Rocky Mountain News, 33, 34, 39, 47
Senior, Edwin W., 11
Sherman Silver Purchase Act, 6, 49, 52
skating rink, 10, 11, 31, 32, 33, 41
sleeper car, 39, 52
strike, 3, 43, 49, 52
Tabor Opera House, 5
Tabor, Horace, 4, 5, 48, 53
The Colorado Daily Chieftain, 36
The Herald Democrat, 1, 14, 15, 19, 20, 21, 22, 36, 37, 55
The Leadville Daily/Evening Chronicle, 42, 43
toboggan, 1, 11, 22, 26, 34, 52
trains, 1, 38, 39, 40, 51, 52
Vaughn, Frank E., 1
warm weather, 17, 19, 41
Wood, Tingley S.
  Director of the Leadville Ice Palace, 11, 12, 14, 17, 19, 20, 26, 30, 33, 34, 41, 43
Wrona, Jeff
  Ice palace model builder, 44

Acknowledgments

Because of my mother, Nancy Banks, I found the story of the Leadville Ice Palace as a teenager. Now I want to make that story come alive for young readers.

Many people helped me bring this book to life. My thanks to Julie VanLaanen and the staff of Filter Press. The staff and volunteers at the Colorado Historic Newspapers Collection, A. J. Brokaw at the Lake County Public Library in Leadville, the staff at the Leadville Heritage Museum, Noah Newman from the Colorado Climate Center at Colorado State University, and my early readers. Finally, a huge thank you to my husband, **John.** He listened to me talk about this story for decades. And he visited Leadville with me so many times. Grateful!

About the Author

Afton Rorvik is a Colorado native. She first went to Leadville as a teenager and spent her allowance money to buy books about Leadville history. She is still reading about Leadville.

Afton has published two non-fiction books for adults, and she has worked as an editor.

She loves to walk and hike in the Colorado sunshine. And she and her husband love to host family and friends around their table. You can learn more about Afton on her website: https://aftonrorvik.com/.

More Now You Know Books

**Bob Sakata:
American Farmer**
ISBN: 978-0-86541-093-0

**Elizabeth Byers:
Denver Pioneer**
ISBN: 978-0-86541-256-9

**Chipeta:
Ute Peacemaker**
ISBN: 978-0-86541-091

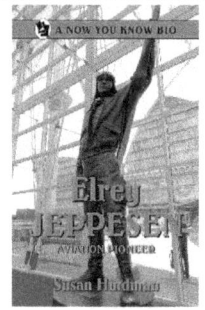

**Elrey Jeppesen:
Aviation Pioneer**
ISBN: 978-0-86541-259-0

**Enos Mills:
Rocky Mountain
Naturalist**
ISBN: 978-0-86541-072-5

**Florence Sabin:
Teacher, Scientist,
Humanitarian**
ISBN: 978-0-86541-139

**General William Palmer:
Railroad Pioneer**
ISBN: 978-0-86541-092-3

**John Denver:
Man for the World**
ISBN: 978-0-86541-088-6

**John Wesley Powell
Soldier, Explorer, Scienti**
ISBN: 978-0-86541-080-

The 1896 Leadville Ice Palace

José Dario Gallegos:
Merchant of the Santa Fe Trail
ISBN: 978-0-86541-084-8

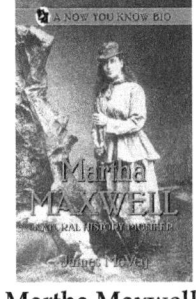

Martha Maxwell:
Natural History Pioneer
ISBN: 978-0-86541-075-6

Mary Elitch Long:
First Lady of Fun
ISBN: 978-0-86541-094-7

Unsinkable: The Molly Brown Story
ISBN: 978-0-86541-081-7

Stephen H. Long:
Frontier Explorer
ISBN: 978-0-86541-250-7

Susan Anderson:
Colorado's Doc Susie
ISBN: 978-0-86541-108-1

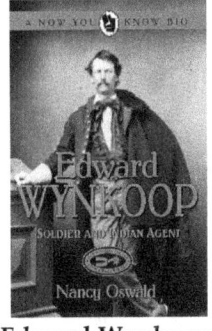

Edward Wynkoop:
Soldier and Indian Agent
ISBN: 978-0-86541-184-5

Justina Ford:
Medical Pioneer
ISBN: 978-0-86541-074-9

Emily Griffith:
Opportunity's Teacher
ISBN: 978-0-86541-077-0

www.ingramcontent.com/pod-product-compliance
Lightning Source LLC
Chambersburg PA
CBHW062104290426
44110CB00022B/2711